7/02

S0-CYE-770

GLEN ROCK PUBLIC LIBRARY
315 ROCK ROAD
GLEN ROCK, N.J. 07452

IT'S
ELECTRIC

ANDREW DUNN

**Illustrated by
ED CARR**

Thomson Learning

New York

Titles in this series
Heat
It's Electric
Lifting by Levers
The Power of Pressure
Simple Slopes
Wheels at Work

First published in the
United States in 1993 by
Thomson Learning
115 Fifth Avenue
New York, NY 10003

First published in 1992 by
Wayland Publishers Ltd.

Copyright © 1992 Wayland Publishers Ltd.

U.S. version copyright © 1993 Thomson Learning

Cataloging-in-Publication Data applied for

ISBN 1-56847-019-3

Printed in Italy

Contents

Words in *italic* in the text are explained in the glossary on page 30.

It's electric

A world powered by electricity

How many times do you switch something on each day? So many things are electric, from tiny devices like doorbells to huge machines like trains.

The lights in your house use electricity, and so does the television, the VCR, the telephone, and the radio. Do you have a calculator or a *quartz* watch? Does your family own a computer or a stereo? These all use electricity.

Imagine your kitchen without a refrigerator, toaster, microwave, or any other electrical gadgets. Electricity produces heat and light, makes motors run, and operates thousands of machines from smoke detectors to *satellites*.

Electricity is quiet, clean, and instant. Only a hundred years ago few homes had electricity; today people depend on it. But what is electricity?

New York is called "The City That Never Sleeps"—thanks mainly to electricity.

Modern homes are full of electrical gadgets.

What is electricity?

Electricity is a form of *energy*. The power of electricity comes from inside tiny particles, called atoms, that make up all things.

The entire world is made of atoms; your own body is made of atoms, as is everything else, from solid rock to the air you breathe.

Atoms

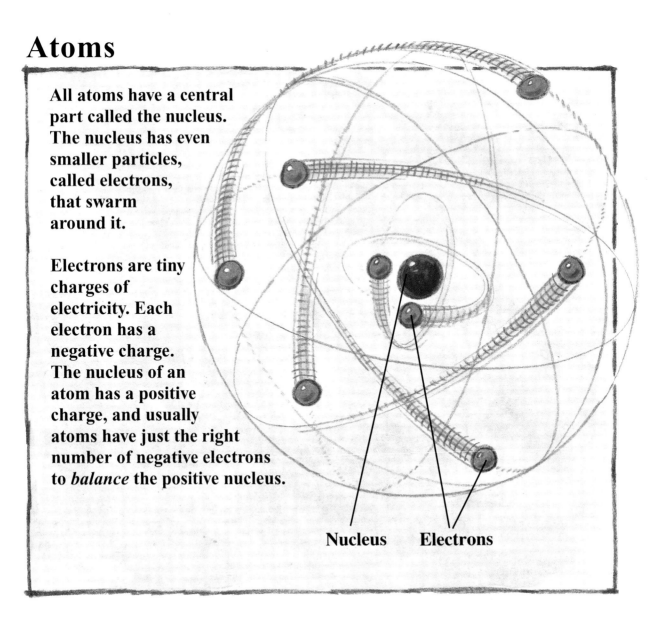

All atoms have a central part called the nucleus. The nucleus has even smaller particles, called electrons, that swarm around it.

Electrons are tiny charges of electricity. Each electron has a negative charge. The nucleus of an atom has a positive charge, and usually atoms have just the right number of negative electrons to *balance* the positive nucleus.

Nucleus   Electrons

Sometimes though, electrons move from one atom to another. This upsets the balance. An atom that loses some of its electrons has a positive charge. An atom with extra electrons has a negative charge.

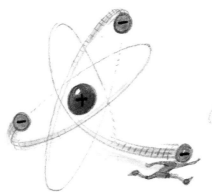

Positive charge: atom has lost an electron.

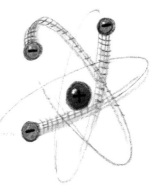

Negative charge: atom has gained an electron.

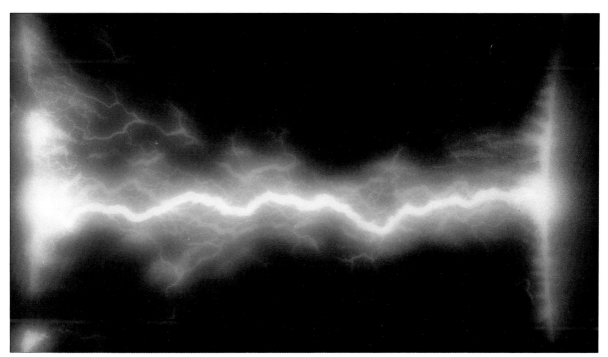

Positive and negative charges always try to balance out. The blue flash of an electric spark is caused by electrons jumping through the air to reach a positive charge.

Static electricity

On a dry day, try rubbing a plastic comb on a piece of wool, like a sweater. Then hold it near your hair (or a friend's hair). The comb *attracts* the hair like a *magnet* attracts metal. However, this pull is not magnetism. The attraction is caused by static electricity.

This kind of electricity is called static because it does not flow—it stays in one place. When the comb and the cloth rub together some electrons rub off the cloth and onto the comb. So the comb has more electrons, which gives it a negative electric charge. The negative

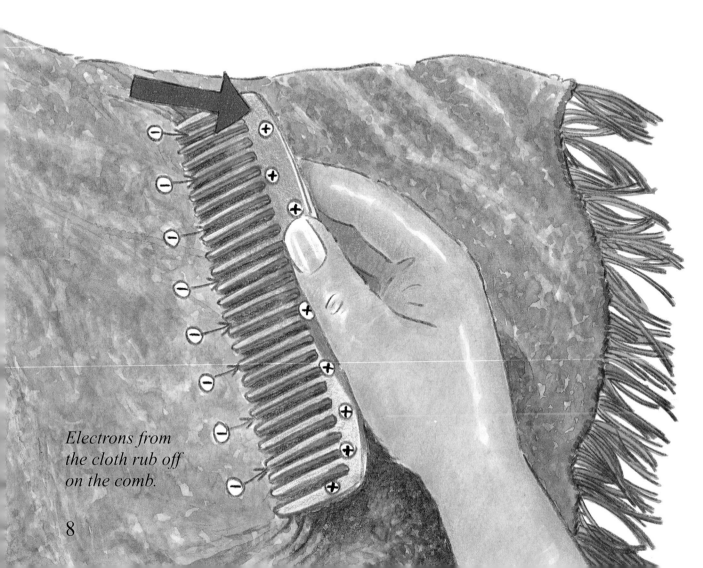

Electrons from the cloth rub off on the comb.

charge draws things with a positive charge toward it.

You can charge yourself with static electricity by rubbing your shoes on a carpet. Then, if you touch something made of metal, you will feel a small shock as the electricity flows away.

Lightning is caused by static electricity. Raindrops moving in clouds can separate positive and negative charges. Most lightning flashes are sparks between one part of a cloud and another, but sometimes the electricity builds up so much that the spark has enough power to reach the ground.

Negative charges on the comb attract positive charges in the hair.

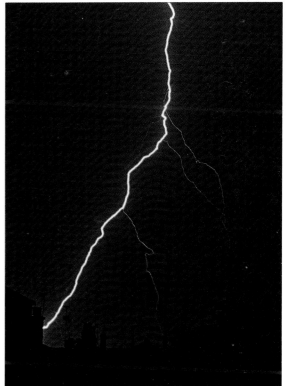

Lightning nearly always strikes tall pointed objects, such as trees, chimneys, or church spires.

Static electricity at work

Electrostatic air filter

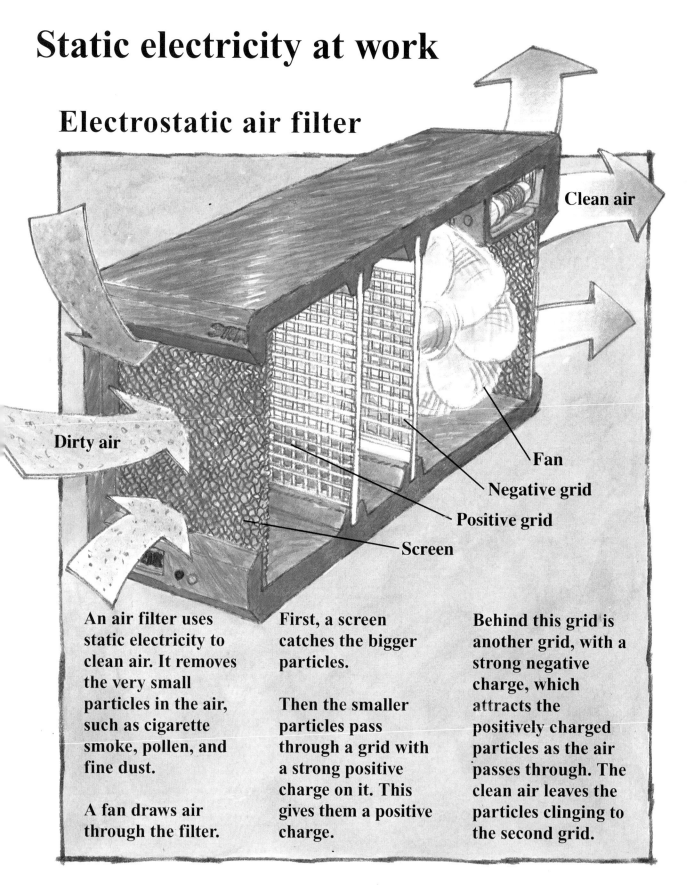

Clean air

Dirty air

Fan

Negative grid

Positive grid

Screen

An air filter uses static electricity to clean air. It removes the very small particles in the air, such as cigarette smoke, pollen, and fine dust.

A fan draws air through the filter.

First, a screen catches the bigger particles.

Then the smaller particles pass through a grid with a strong positive charge on it. This gives them a positive charge.

Behind this grid is another grid, with a strong negative charge, which attracts the positively charged particles as the air passes through. The clean air leaves the particles clinging to the second grid.

Photocopier

The attraction of static electricity is also used by high-speed photocopiers.

Inside a photocopier there is a metal drum with a negative charge.

A lamp passes over the paper being copied, shining on whatever is written or drawn on it. *Lenses* project a reflected image onto the drum as it turns.

Where light hits the drum, the electric charge disappears, so the only parts still charged are where the original paper was dark.

Then ink powder, called toner, is poured onto the drum. The ink only sticks to the charged areas. So when the drum rolls over a new sheet of paper, it makes an exact copy of the original image.

1 Drum has negative charge.

2 Lamp and lens project image on to drum.

3 Toner powder sticks to charged areas.

4 Drum rolls over paper.

Photocopiers have replaced messy, smudgy copiers that used wet chemicals.

Electricity on the move

The electricity we use most is not static, but flows in a current. Current electricity makes light bulbs glow and motors turn.

An electric current is made of electrons moving along a conductor. A conductor is any material that allows electrons to move along it, such as metal. Many materials, however, such as wood, plastic, and stone, do not conduct electricity. They are called insulators.

To make a current flow, there must be something to push the electrons and keep them moving. One simple source of this energy is a "wet" battery, which uses a *chemical reaction*.

Wet-cell battery

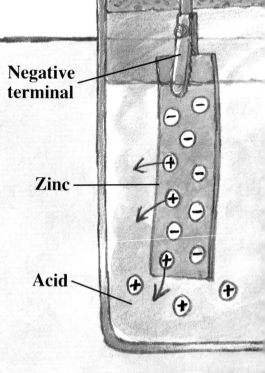

When two types of metal, such as zinc and copper, are put into a jar of *acid* and connected by a wire, a reaction starts.

The acid takes electrons from the copper. At the same time, positively charged zinc atoms go into the acid, leaving electrons behind.

So electrons travel from the zinc (the "negative *terminal*") through the wire to the copper (the "positive terminal").

During the reaction, the zinc changes. Eventually no pure zinc is left, so the current stops.

Negative terminal

Zinc

Acid

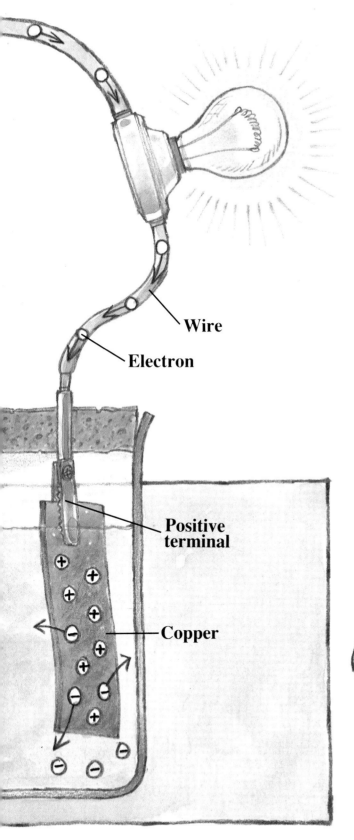

Wire

Electron

Positive
terminal

Copper

Car battery

A car battery contains several *cells*. It uses different metals in sulfuric acid to produce a current strong enough to start the car. When the car is running, a generator feeds a current back into the battery. This makes the reaction go backward, which recharges the battery. This battery contains six cells connected together.

Plug
to
cells

Cells

Batteries and circuits

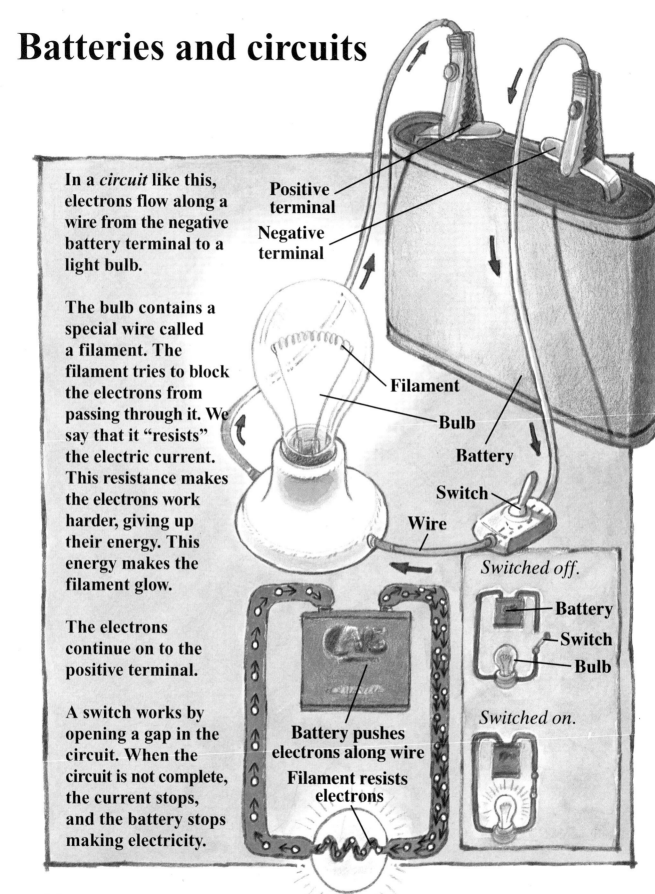

In a *circuit* like this, electrons flow along a wire from the negative battery terminal to a light bulb.

The bulb contains a special wire called a filament. The filament tries to block the electrons from passing through it. We say that it "resists" the electric current. This resistance makes the electrons work harder, giving up their energy. This energy makes the filament glow.

The electrons continue on to the positive terminal.

A switch works by opening a gap in the circuit. When the circuit is not complete, the current stops, and the battery stops making electricity.

Positive terminal

Negative terminal

Filament

Bulb

Battery

Switch

Wire

Battery pushes electrons along wire

Filament resists electrons

Switched off.

Battery

Switch

Bulb

Switched on.

Dry-cell battery

The batteries you use every day are not full of acid. Still, they need something similar.

In "dry" batteries, the acid is replaced by a damp paste of chemical powders.

The battery case is made of zinc and connected to the negative terminal. Down the center of the battery is a rod made of carbon, connected to the positive terminal.

A flashlight battery is a dry-cell battery. The flashlight is switched on by closing a gap in the circuit. Then, electrons go from the zinc case, through the circuit, and to the carbon rod. The current moves from the negative to the positive terminal.

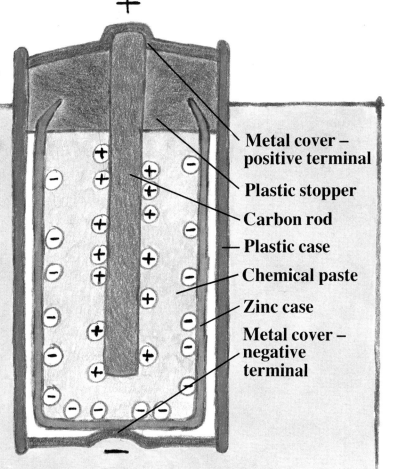

Metal cover – positive terminal

Plastic stopper

Carbon rod

Plastic case

Chemical paste

Zinc case

Metal cover – negative terminal

The moist, gray paste is wrapped around the carbon rod between rolls of paper.

Household current

The current produced by a battery flows in only one direction—from the negative terminal to the positive. This is called a direct current (DC).

The electric current that flows from plug sockets in homes and offices is different. Because of the way household electricity is made, the current keeps changing direction. It is an alternating current (AC). The electrons move back and forth, 60 times every second. The terminals change from positive to negative and back again just as quickly.

A light bulb lights up whichever

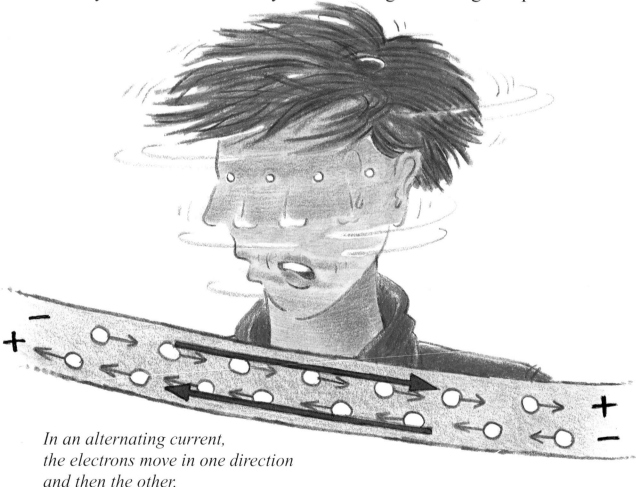

In an alternating current, the electrons move in one direction and then the other.

way the current flows, so it does not matter that household current is an alternating current.

Alternating current is produced in large power plants. It is carried to its user through either underground cables or cables hung between poles. For safety, it is important that the cables be somewhere people and animals cannot get to easily. Unlike electricity from a flashlight battery, electricity from a socket is very powerful. It can give you a bad shock and burn you. It can even kill you. **Never touch an electrical outlet, and never play with household current.**

Powerful electricity generated at the power plant is carried where it is needed by thick cables hung from pylons.

Energy from light

Most electricity is produced from chemical energy, whether in a battery or from burning fuel at a power plant. However, there are other ways of generating electricity.

Sunlight can be turned into electricity by solar cells. Enormous panels of solar cells are used to power space satellites. On Earth, they are most useful in sunny places that are not connected to power lines.

This calculator has tiny solar cells. Behind it are much larger solar cells used to power machinery.

Solar cell

Solar cells are made of materials called semiconductors. These can behave either like conductors or like insulators. In solar cells they produce electricity when light falls on them.

Different types of semiconductors are arranged in layers in a solar cell. When light falls on the cell, it knocks electrons off some of the atoms. As the electrons move to a different layer, they make an electric current.

Each cell has negative and positive terminals, just like a battery.

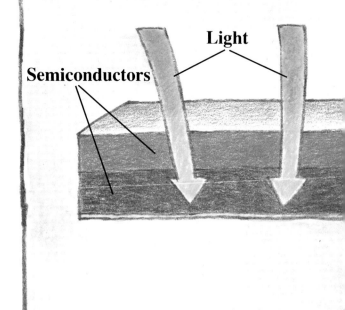

18

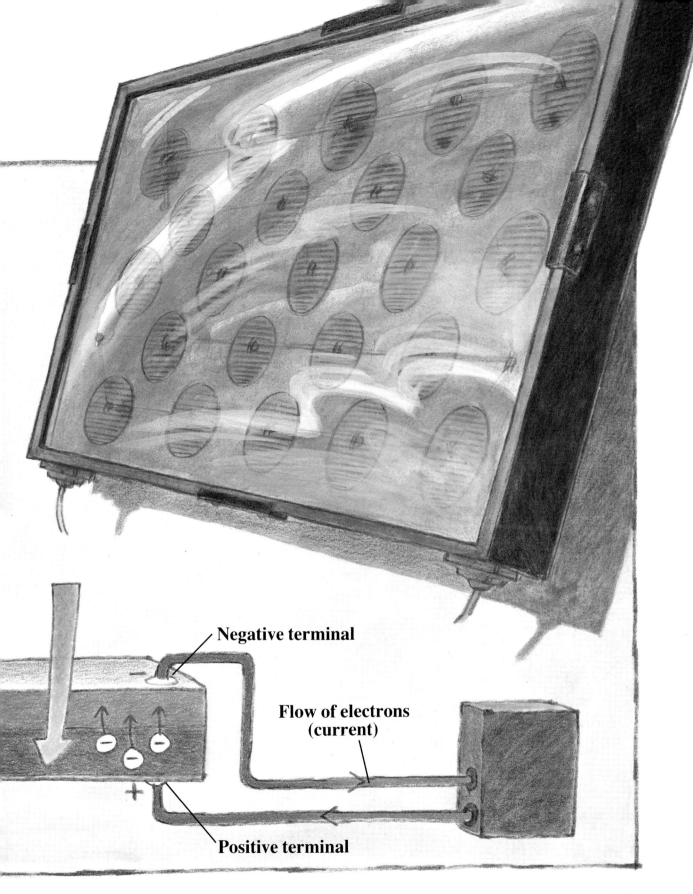

Negative terminal

**Flow of electrons
(current)**

+

Positive terminal

Magnetism

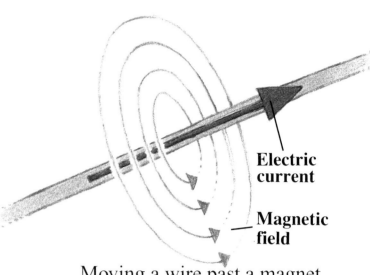

Electric current

Magnetic field

Electricity and magnetism cannot be separated. Where there is an electric current, there is always a magnetic field.

An electric current flowing through a wire produces magnetism around it. Put a magnetic compass near a wire carrying current from a battery and see what happens!

The opposite is also true.

Moving a wire past a magnet produces an electric current in the wire.

So magnetism can be used to make electricity, and electricity to make magnets.

Electromagnets

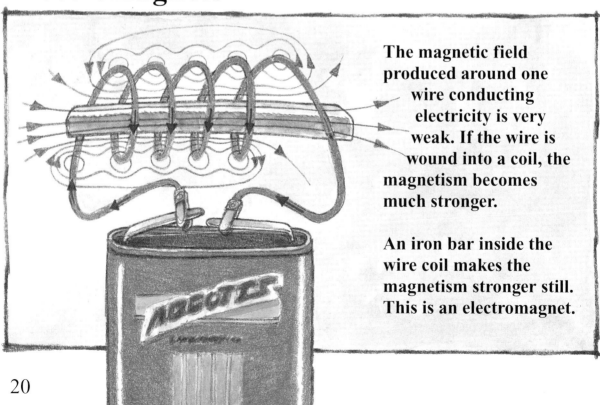

The magnetic field produced around one wire conducting electricity is very weak. If the wire is wound into a coil, the magnetism becomes much stronger.

An iron bar inside the wire coil makes the magnetism stronger still. This is an electromagnet.

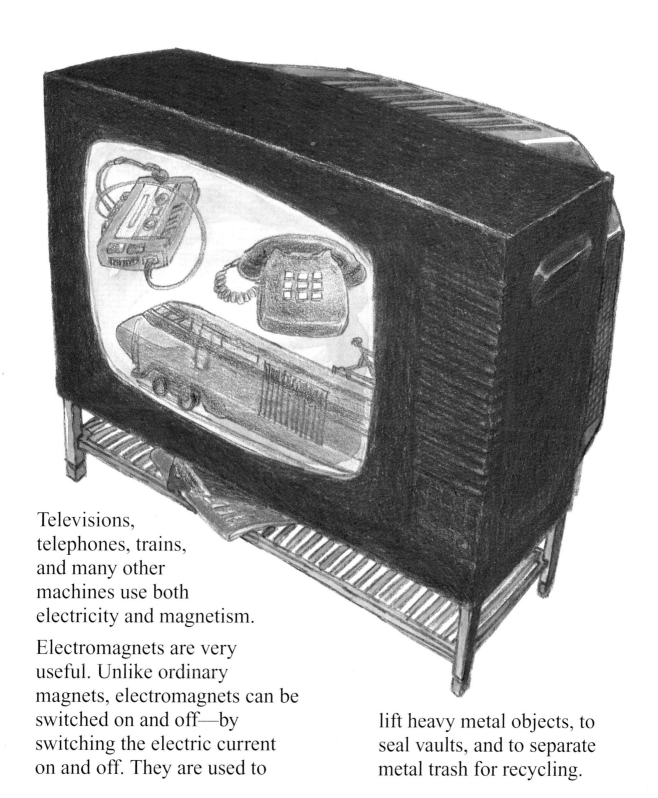

Televisions, telephones, trains, and many other machines use both electricity and magnetism.

Electromagnets are very useful. Unlike ordinary magnets, electromagnets can be switched on and off—by switching the electric current on and off. They are used to lift heavy metal objects, to seal vaults, and to separate metal trash for recycling.

Electromagnets in action

Doorbells

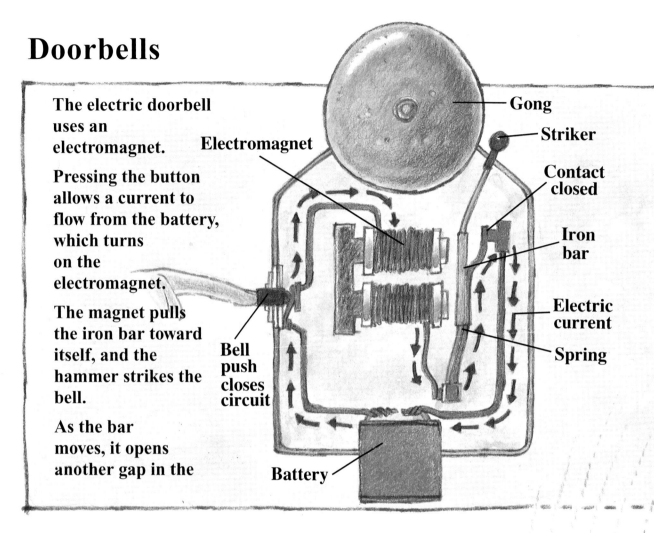

The electric doorbell uses an electromagnet.

Pressing the button allows a current to flow from the battery, which turns on the electromagnet.

The magnet pulls the iron bar toward itself, and the hammer strikes the bell.

As the bar moves, it opens another gap in the

Electromagnet

Gong

Striker

Contact closed

Iron bar

Electric current

Spring

Bell push closes circuit

Battery

Loudspeakers

Behind the cone of a loudspeaker is a coil of wire surrounded by an ordinary magnet.

An electric current, carrying the pattern of the sound *vibrations,* passes through the coil. As it does so, the coil produces a vibrating magnetic field based on the sound pattern.

Magnetic attraction and *repulsion* between this magnetic field and the ordinary magnet make the coil move. This moves the cone, which makes the air vibrate, producing sound!

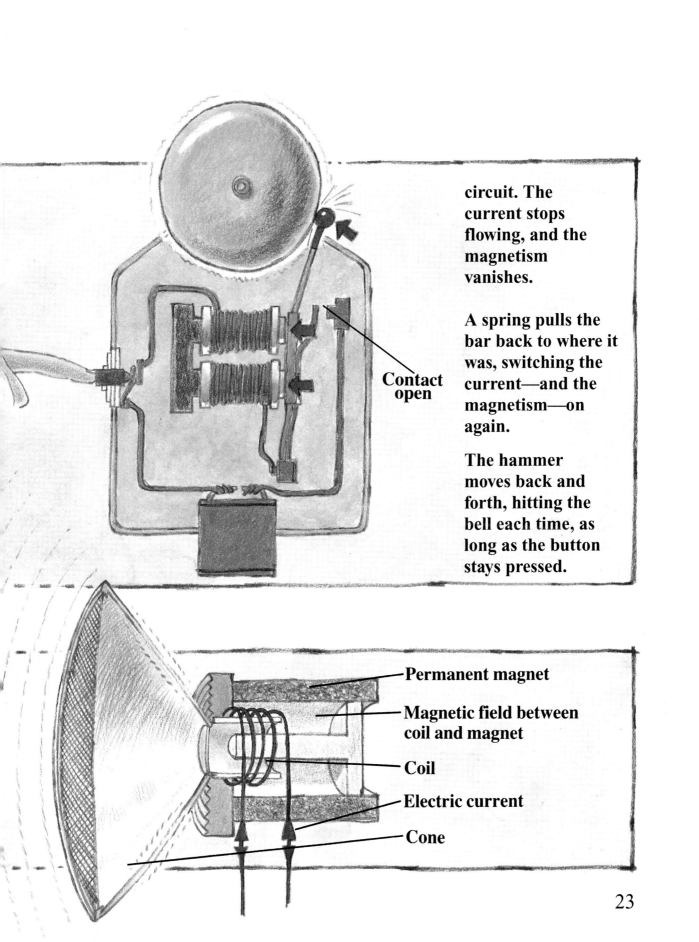

circuit. The current stops flowing, and the magnetism vanishes.

A spring pulls the bar back to where it was, switching the current—and the magnetism—on again.

The hammer moves back and forth, hitting the bell each time, as long as the button stays pressed.

Contact open

Permanent magnet

Magnetic field between coil and magnet

Coil

Electric current

Cone

The electric motor

The electric motor is one of the most useful machines there is. It can be very large or very small. It can run anything from portable radios to powerful high-speed trains.

One simple type of motor runs on direct current from a battery. The current flows through a coil that spins between the two *poles*, north and south, of a magnet (see the illustration on page 25).

The force of a magnet goes from the north pole to the south pole. North and south poles always attract each other. Two north poles or two south poles will always *repel* each other.

The magnetic field produced by the coil in the motor lines up with the field between the two poles of the magnet, and they repel each other. Just like two north poles repel each other, the coil is repelled and turns to move out of the way.

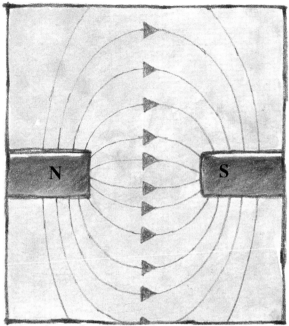

North and south poles attract.

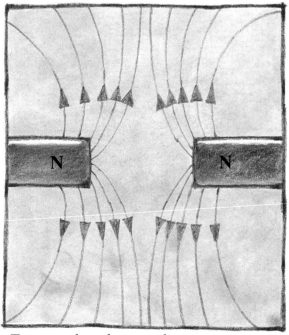

Two north poles repel.

The coil is attached to a device called a commutator. The commutator conducts electricity to the coil, even when it is turning, by using wire brushes as contacts. At every half-turn, the commutator changes the direction of the current going through the coil. As a result, the direction of the coil's magnetic field also changes. At every half-turn the coil is again repelled by the magnet, and so keeps on spinning.

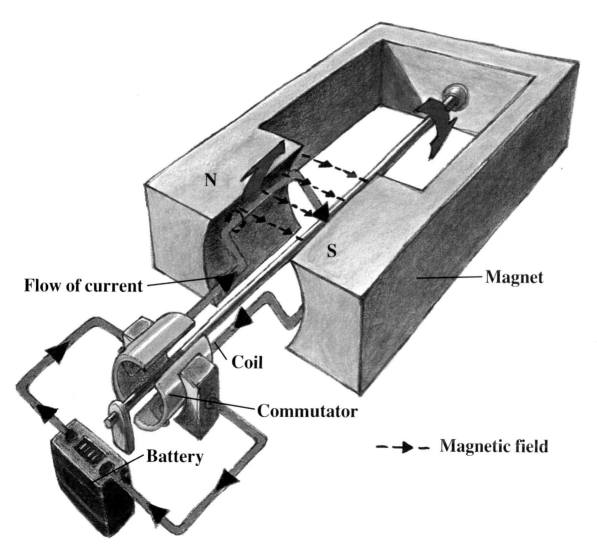

N

S

Flow of current

Coil

Commutator

Battery

Magnet

– ➤ – **Magnetic field**

Generating electricity

An electric generator is very similar to an electric motor—but in reverse. Instead of using electricity and a magnet to make a coil spin, it uses a spinning coil and a magnet to make electricity.

Electricity is produced in power plants at a very high voltage, using large coils and powerful magnets. Voltage is a measurement for the amount of force moving the electrons in an electric current.

At high voltage, much less energy is lost as the electricity is carried through long power lines. Near homes and offices, the voltage is reduced to a lower voltage for ordinary use. This voltage varies from country to country. In the United States and Canada the standard for household current is 110 volts. In Britain and Australia it is 240 volts. Appliances in one country cannot always be used with another country's voltage.

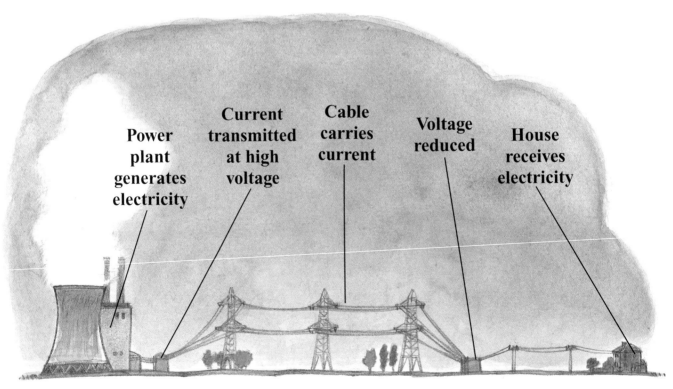

Power plant generates electricity

Current transmitted at high voltage

Cable carries current

Voltage reduced

House receives electricity

The generator

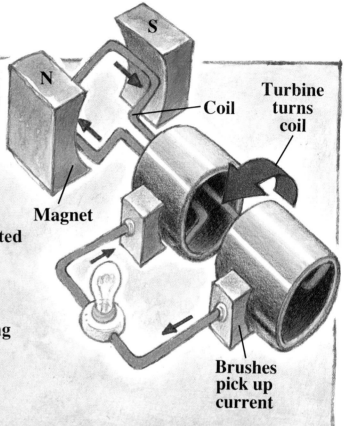

As the coil spins between the poles of the magnet, electricity flows through its wires.

Every time the coil turns halfway, the current changes direction. This is one reason why household current is alternating current. In the United States, generators spin 60 times every second.

The generating coil is usually turned by a steam *turbine*, using steam made by heat from coal, oil, gas, or nuclear reaction.

N **S**

Coil

Turbine turns coil

Magnet

Brushes pick up current

This generator uses a turbine driven by nuclear power.

The magic of electricity

So much of the world now relies on electricity that you may not even realize it. All the time, millions upon millions of electrons are flowing through wires all around you—not just in moving machinery, but also in the electronic *microchips* that tell computers what to do.

Every year computers become smaller, faster, and more powerful. They are already doing many tasks that humans used to do. People depend on computers more and more in hospitals, stores, businesses, and even in homes. New discoveries about electronics will continue to change the way people live. It is amazing to think that all these changes spring from the power of the tiny electron.

Look at all the machines in this picture that need electricity to make them work.

Glossary

Acid A kind of liquid that can burn your skin. Lemon juice is a weak acid.

Attract Pull without touching, or make something come nearer.

Balance Equality between two things.

Cell (of battery) A container with chemicals in it for making electricity. A flashlight battery has just one cell. A car battery has several.

Chemical reaction A process in which the molecules of two or more substances change. Their atoms are rearranged, producing different substances.

Circuit A loop of wires and other objects that conduct electricity, connected so that an electric current will flow through it.

Energy The power needed to do something.

Lenses Pieces of curved glass or plastic that can make beams of light bend. Eyeglasses and cameras contain lenses.

Magnet An object that can pull, or attract, things made of iron, steel, and other metals.

Microchips Tiny parts used in electronic machines such as computers. They have tiny electrical circuits printed on them that can process and use information by changing electronic signals.

Poles The two ends of a magnet.

Quartz A hard, glasslike material found in some kinds of rock. It is used in watches and clocks, because electricity from a battery makes the quartz vibrate at a very regular rate.

Repel Force something away.

Repulsion A force that drives things apart.

Satellite Anything that travels around a planet in space. Artificial satellites are machines put in space by people. They can relay television pictures and telephone messages around the world and send information about the weather back to Earth.

Terminal One of the two points on a battery where the electric current goes in or out.

Turbine A machine that uses the power of steam, gas, or water to make a shaft turn around. Turbines are often used in power plants.

Vibrations Very quick back-and-forth movements. Sound is made by air particles vibrating.

Books to read

Ardley, Neil. *Electricity*. New York: Macmillan, 1992.

Asimov, Isaac. *How Did We Find Out About Electricity?*
New York: Walker & Co, 1973.

Bailey, Mark W. *Electricity*. Milwaukee: Raintree Steck-Vaughn, 1988.

Bains, Rae. *Discovering Electricity*. Mahwah, N.J.: Troll, 1982.

Cosner, Sharon *The Light Bulb: Inventions That Changed Our Lives*.
New York: Walker & Co., 1984.

Gutnick, Martin J. *Electricity: From Faraday to Solar Generators*.
New York: Franklin Watts, 1986.

Math, Irwin. *Wires and Watts: Using and Understanding Electricity*.
New York: Macmillan, 1989.

Picture acknowledgments

The publishers would like to thank the following for providing the
photographs for this book: Chapel Studios 11; Eye Ubiquitous 4
(P. Thompson); Science Photo Library 4 (P. Jude), 9 (S. Stammers),
15 (J. Burgess), 18 (M. Bond), 27 (A. Bartel); Zefa 17 (Rossenbach).

Index